# Parenting Teens with PTSD

*Parenting Children through Trauma and Promoting Healing-A Successful Parenting Guide*

## Baz Hicks

**Copyright 2023 by Baz Hicks**

All rights reserved. No part of this book may be reproduced, stored in a retrieval system, or transmitted in any form or by any means, electronic, mechanical, photocopying, recording, or otherwise, without the prior written permission of the copyright owner.

# Table of contents

Introduction ..................................................... 5

Understanding the Impact of PTSD on Teenagers
............................................................................ 7

The Importance of Parental Support and Guidance ............................................................... 9

Chapter 1 ......................................................... 13

    Understanding post-traumatic stress disorder
............................................................................ 13

Chapter 2 ......................................................... 23

    Common Triggers and Stressors .................. 23

Chapter 3 ......................................................... 31

    Helping a Kid with PTSD ............................ 31

Chapter 4 ......................................................... 41

    Discipline a Child with PTSD: Challenges, what to Avoid and What to Do ..................... 41

Chapter 5 ......................................................... 47

    Effective Parenting Strategies for Teens with PTSD ............................................................ 47

Chapter 6 ......................................................... 57

Tips for Teachers ........................................... 57
Chapter 7 .......................................................... 67
The Aftermath of PTSD In Children ........... 67

## Introduction

Like adults, children may acquire PTSD after witnessing a terrible experience. With the correct help, children may begin to recover from their trauma.

If your child has recently had a trauma, you could notice that they appear withdrawn or that memories or nightmares are tormenting them. They could look disconnected, startle easily, or be particularly clinging. You could worry whether they're displaying indications of post-traumatic stress disorder (PTSD).

Traumatic situations may have a severe physical and emotional influence on our minds and bodies. The body goes into fight, flight, or freeze mode as a technique of dealing with threats. In other situations, the body isn't entirely able to recover from the acute stress condition, resulting in the symptoms that make up PTSD.

When left unresolved, the emotional and physical impacts of childhood trauma may endure throughout adulthood. In fact, adverse childhood experiences (ACEs)Trusted Source — such as assault, abuse, or neglect — that occur before age 17 might contribute to several chronic health issues, mental illness, and drug use disorders in adulthood.

The good news is that early intervention may considerably enhance a child's growth and capacity to recover and flourish. Noticing the signs and getting help are the first steps.

Children may encounter trauma from various angles. Natural calamities damage communities, leaving families homeless. Children are caught in the crossfire of shootings and neighborhood violence. But the fiercest emotional storms—neglect and abuse—rage within the house, where children are meant to feel secure and cherished. Even while adults suffer trauma, too, age helps them absorb the experiences more successfully and return to a feeling of normality. For children, early-life experiences may truly affect their young brains and result in developmental and behavioral disorders.

Without a deep, caring connection with parents and other caregivers, children learn they cannot depend on anybody to aid them. When they are used and mistreated, youngsters think that they are evil and the world is dangerous and dreadful. Trauma disrupts the normal development of the brain and neurological system, the immune system, and the body's stress response systems.

## Understanding the Impact of PTSD on Teenagers

Teenagers, in the middle of their growth years, are already undergoing tremendous physical, emotional, and cognitive changes. When PTSD enters the scene, these developmental problems might be further worsened. PTSD in teens sometimes arises from a broad variety of stressful situations such as physical or sexual abuse, neglect, witnessing violence, accidents, or natural catastrophes. The effect of trauma on teenagers may be substantial since their brains are still growing and their coping systems are not yet completely evolved.

One of the key symptoms of PTSD is the re-experiencing of traumatic experiences via intrusive thoughts, nightmares, or flashbacks. For teens, these stressful events may disturb their everyday life, impairing their focus, sleep habits, and general mental well-being. Consequently, their academic performance may deteriorate, and they may find it difficult to establish good connections with classmates and family members. Additionally, teens with PTSD may demonstrate behavioral changes such as impatience, rage, violence, or withdrawal.

It is vital for parents to acknowledge the special issues experienced by teens with PTSD. Their problems could emerge differently compared to adults or younger children.

Adolescents may struggle with self-identity, self-esteem, and social integration, and these concerns may be further compounded when PTSD is present. Understanding the individual effect of PTSD on teens helps parents to give targeted assistance and therapies that meet their unique needs.

## The Importance of Parental Support and Guidance

When teens encounter the overwhelming consequences of PTSD, the role of parents becomes important in their rehabilitation and healing process. Parental support and assistance offer a key anchor for teens as they navigate through the problems of PTSD. By establishing a secure and loving atmosphere, parents may develop a foundation of trust and understanding, allowing their teenagers to seek comfort and aid when required.

One of the main way's parents may assist their kids with PTSD is by actively listening and acknowledging their experiences. It is crucial for parents to offer room for open and non-judgmental conversation, enabling their teenagers to share their ideas, worries, and feelings.

Listening carefully and validating their emotions helps kids feel understood, recognized, and supported, which may have a dramatic beneficial influence on their well-being.

In addition to emotional support, parents may give practical counsel to help youngsters handle the problems of PTSD. Establishing routines and limits may give stability and a feeling of security in their everyday life. Consistency and routine may be especially useful for teens with PTSD since it provides them with a feeling of predictability in an otherwise chaotic environment.

Parents may also take an active part in their teen's treatment and recovery by providing access to expert care. Seeking treatment choices particularly suited to teenagers with PTSD may give crucial assistance and strategies for managing symptoms and encouraging recovery. Collaborating with mental health specialists may also offer parents a greater knowledge of their teenager's situation and equip them with appropriate tools to help their recovery path.

Furthermore, parents may educate themselves about PTSD, its symptoms, and accessible therapies. This understanding helps parents to have educated dialogues with their adolescents, offering factual information and removing any misconceptions or stigmas linked with mental health disorders. By being well-informed and educated, parents can successfully advocate for their teenager's needs and ensure they get the right care and support.

Parental care goes beyond the acute treatment of PTSD. It also entails helping teens build appropriate coping skills and resilience. Parents may aid their teenagers in learning and practicing stress management skills, such as deep breathing exercises, mindfulness, or participating in creative outlets like painting or writing. Encouraging self-care activities, such as indulging in hobbies, obtaining regular exercise, and keeping a healthy lifestyle, may also add to their overall well-being.

Building a solid support network is equally vital for parents and teens alike. Connecting with other families who have gone through similar circumstances may create a feeling of connection and understanding. Support groups or online forums devoted to parents and teens struggling with PTSD may serve as helpful platforms for sharing experiences, exchanging information, and obtaining support from people who genuinely appreciate the issues.

While offering support and advice, it is vital for parents to find a balance between being active and leaving their adolescents room for individuality. Teenagers need chances to develop their independence and decision-making abilities, even when suffering from PTSD. Encouraging their involvement in age-appropriate activities and progressively allowing them to make decisions enhances their feeling of agency and self-confidence.

Lastly, parents must emphasize their own self-care. Caring for a teenager with PTSD may be emotionally draining and physically tiring. Engaging in self-care behaviors, such as seeking support from friends and family, following personal hobbies, and getting professional assistance if required, assists parents to preserve their own well-being. By taking care of themselves, parents may better assist their teenager's road to recovery.

## Chapter 1

# Understanding post-traumatic stress disorder

Post-traumatic stress disorder (PTSD) is a debilitating illness that follows an incident that the individual finds horrifying, either physically or emotionally, leading the person who experienced the event to have persistent, fearful thoughts and recollections, or flashbacks, of the encounter.

Sometimes repercussions from the traumatic events might be delayed for 6 months or more, but when PTSD begins quickly after an incident, the condition normally fades within 3 months. Some persons with PTSD have long-term repercussions and may feel persistent, and emotionally numb. PTSD in children frequently develops as a chronic condition.

## The causes post-traumatic stress disorder

The event(s) that initiates PTSD may be:

Something that happened in the person's life.

Something that happened in the life of someone close to him or her.

Something the individual observed.

The proximity and relationship of the child to the trauma, the severity of the trauma, the length of the traumatic event, the repetition of the traumatic event, the child's resilience, the child's coping mechanisms, and the resources available to the child from the family and community after the event(s) all influence the child's risk for developing PTSD.

The following are some instances of occurrences when there is a danger of damage or death that may trigger PTSD whether experienced or observed as a kid or adolescent:

Serious accidents (such as automobile or rail collisions)

Invasive medical treatments for young children (under the age of 6)

Animal bites (such as dog bites)

Natural calamities (such as floods or earthquakes)

Man-made calamities (such as bombs)

Violent personal assaults (such as a mugging, rape, torture, being kept hostage, or abduction)

Physical abuse

Sexual assault

Sexual molestation

Emotional abuse, bullying

Neglect

## Who is impacted by post-traumatic stress disorder?

About 4% of children under age 18 are exposed to some sort of trauma throughout their lives that leads to post-traumatic stress disorder. According to the National Institute of Mental Health, among those children and adolescents who have suffered trauma, roughly 7% of females and 2% of boys are diagnosed with PTSD.

## Symptoms of PTSD in children

Trauma may lead to a broad variety of mental, emotional, and behavioral symptoms. Many of the symptoms of PTSD in adults also emerge in children, adolescents, and teenagers.

It might take some time after an occurrence for the consequences of trauma to show themselves. If they emerge shortly after an incident, the symptoms normally improve around 3 months. Sometimes, the impacts cannot show up for 6 months or longer after the experience occurred.

For a diagnosis of PTSD, the youngster will have had disruptive symptoms for at least 1 month.

**Typical symptoms of PTSD in kids include:**

Flashbacks or sensations as though the tragedy is occurring again

Looking anxious, agitated, or overly attentive, also known as hypervigilance

Looking "out of it," disconnected, or in a daze with unwanted thoughts or recollections regarding the distressing event trouble sleeping, including nightmares

Avoidance of people, places, objects, or circumstances that are reminders of the traumatic event problems in school no longer enjoying activities they used to intense outbursts of rage or sadness unexplained health issues, such as headaches or stomach discomfort

Fears about dying or being hurt regressive habits, such as thumb-sucking or bed-wetting

Adolescents or teenagers could resort to substance usages, such as alcohol or drugs, to cope with the trauma and its repercussions.

**Children with PTSD often encounter three sorts of symptoms:**

### Re-experiencing the trauma

The youngster continues to mentally re-live the painful situation, over and over again.

He may have "flashbacks" of the incident, feeling that he is really going through the experience again. He may even imagine pictures, sounds, or scents from the incident.

He may have terrible nightmares (either about the traumatic incident or about other terrifying things).

He may feel the urge to "hash out" the situation orally or in play.

He cannot stop thinking about the horrible incident, no matter what he does.

### Avoidance

The youngster consciously avoids any idea, object, location, or scenario that is connected to the traumatic experience or reminds him of the incident in any way.

He may have difficulties recalling specifics about the experience ("blocking it out").

He may grow numb to his sensations and environment in general as a coping tactic.

**Increased agitation**

The youngster feels as if he must continuously be "on guard," in case the trauma occurs again or another risky circumstance develops.

He could be easily surprised or terrified.

He may have problems falling or staying asleep.

He may suffer difficulties focusing on academics and other normal duties.

He could experience episodes of unjustified or excessive wrath.

A very young kid who cannot communicate emotions or ideas regarding a trauma may display the following after the experience:

out-of-control, disruptive conduct

great anxiety about being removed from the main caregiver

**What are some of the incidents that might trigger PTSD in children?**

While any stressful experience might lead a kid to acquire PTSD, the illness most typically stems from:

being assaulted physically while watching domestic abuse A major injury or being engaged in a serious accident, as well as seeing or experiencing a violent incident in a classroom or in the community (such as a shooting at a school).

**A kid suffers PTSD when:**

he regards the encounter as life-threatening or highly dangerous he reacts to the situation with profound dread, helplessness, or terror

Treatment for PTSD is complicated, and continuous and relies very lot on the child's specific symptoms and circumstances. However, psychotherapy "(talk therapy"), family support, and—in some cases—the inclusion of the medicine in the treatment program have all demonstrated outstanding success in helping youngsters with PTSD return to a normal, healthy existence.

**How is post-traumatic stress disorder diagnosed?**

Not every kid or teenager who endures trauma gets PTSD. Only when symptoms persist for more than a month and have a noticeable effect on the child's functioning and quality of life is PTSD recognized. If a person has PTSD, symptoms often appear 3 months after the trauma, however they might appear months or years afterwards.

Childhood can be the onset age for PTSD, and it may be accompanied by:

Childhood can be the onset age for PTSD, and it may be accompanied by:

Depression

Substance abuse

Anxiety

The duration of the condition varies. Some individuals heal within 6 months, others have symptoms that persist much longer.

A child psychiatrist or other trained mental health practitioner generally diagnoses PTSD in children or adolescents after a full psychiatric assessment. Parents who observe signs of PTSD in their kid or adolescent may benefit by getting an examination early. Early treatment may reduce future issues.

## Chapter 2

## Common Triggers and Stressors

Understanding the frequent triggers and stresses that may increase symptoms of PTSD in teens is vital in building a supportive and safe environment. Triggers are external or internal cues that remind people of the traumatic incident, prompting uncomfortable feelings and physiological reactions.

Common external triggers for teens with PTSD might include events or surroundings evocative of the trauma, such as loud sounds, crowded rooms, or particular locations. Certain odors, noises, or even certain dates may potentially operate as triggers. Additionally, watching or hearing about comparable traumatic occurrences in the media or in their society might worsen their symptoms.

Internal triggers relate to thoughts, feelings, or physiological sensations that remind youngsters of the traumatic incident. For example, thoughts of dread, grief, anger, or anxiety might act as internal triggers for teens with PTSD. Certain thoughts or memories related to the event might also stimulate their symptoms. It is crucial for parents, caregivers, and educators to be aware of these triggers and work jointly with teens to build appropriate coping mechanisms to control and reduce their effects.

In addition to triggers, teens with PTSD may also endure ordinary stresses that may increase their symptoms. Adolescence itself may be a period of heightened stress owing to academic expectations, peer connections, and the process of self-discovery. These pressures, along with the problems of PTSD, may produce a more intense and overwhelming experience for teens.

Family interactions may also contribute to stress levels. Adolescents with PTSD may need more help and understanding from their family members. Conflict, instability, or a lack of emotional support within the family setting might further damage their well-being and healing. It is vital for parents and caregivers to provide a loving and supportive culture that fosters open communication and encourages teens to seek help when required.

Furthermore, the act of seeking treatment or participating in therapy may be a stressor in itself. Teenagers may suffer worry, reluctance, or terror connected with talking and reliving their painful experiences. It is crucial for parents, caregivers, and mental health professionals to approach therapy with empathy and patience, ensuring that teens feel secure and supported throughout the treatment process.

By recognizing the unique challenges faced by teenagers with PTSD, including the impact on identity formation, social dynamics, academic performance, and the presence of triggers and stressors, parents, caregivers, and educators can adopt a proactive approach to support and assist teenagers in their journey towards healing and recovery.

## How is PTSD addressed in children and adolescents?

Although some children demonstrate a natural remission of PTSD symptoms over a period of a few months, a large proportion of children continue to display symptoms for years if untreated. Trauma Focused psychotherapies have the strongest scientific backing for children and adolescents.

### Cognitive-Behavioral Therapy (CBT)

Cognitive-Behavioral Therapy (CBT) Research studies demonstrate that CBT is the most effective strategy for treating children. The therapy with the greatest empirical evidence is Trauma-Focused CBT (TF-CBT). TF-CBT often involves the child directly addressing the traumatic incident (exposure), anxiety management strategies such as relaxation and assertiveness training, and correction of erroneous or distorted trauma-related beliefs.

Although there is a considerable dispute surrounding exposing children to the events that fear them, exposure-based therapies tend to be most relevant when memories or reminders of the trauma disturb the kid. Children may be introduced progressively and taught relaxation so that they can learn to relax while remembering their experiences. Through this method, people realize that they do not have to be terrified of their memories.

CBT also entails correcting children's incorrect ideas such as, "The world is totally unsafe." The majority of research has concluded that it is safe and helpful to utilize CBT for children with PTSD.

CBT is commonly complemented by psycho-education and parental participation. Psycho-education is education regarding PTSD symptoms and their impact. It is as crucial for parents and caregivers to understand the impacts of PTSD as it is for children. Rescarch suggests that the more parents deal with the trauma, and the more they help their children, the better their children will function. Therefore, it is crucial for parents to get therapy for themselves in order to acquire the required coping skills that will aid their children.

## Play therapy

Play therapy may be used to help young children with PTSD who are not able to cope with the trauma more directly. The therapist employs games, drawings, and other strategies to help the youngsters process their terrible experiences.

## Psychological First Aid

Psychological First Aid has been utilized for school-aged children and adolescents exposed to catastrophes and community violence and may be applied in schools and traditional settings. Psychological First Aid entails offering comfort and support, normalizing the children's behaviors, helping caregivers cope with changes in the child's emotions and behavior, teaching calming and problem-solving skills, and recommending the most symptomatic children for further treatment. Learn more about Psychological First Aid.

## Eye Movement Desensitization and Reprocessing (EMDR)

Another technique, EMDR, combines cognitive therapy with guided eye movements. While EMDR has been found to be successful in treating adults, research on children is not as robust. Studies reveal that it is the cognitive component rather than the eye movements that accounts for the shift.

## Medications

Selective serotonin reuptake inhibitors (SSRIs) are licensed for usage in individuals with PTSD. SSRIs are licensed for use in children and adolescents with depression and OCD. Preliminary research shows SSRIs may be useful in treating PTSD, yet there may also be dangers such as irritability, poor sleep, and inattention. At this time, there is inadequate data to support the usage of SSRIs.

**Specialized Interventions**

Specialized therapies may be essential for children demonstrating extremely troublesome symptoms or behaviors, such as improper sexual activities, serious behavioral issues, or drug misuse.

## Chapter 3

## Helping a Kid with PTSD

As a parent or caregiver, supporting a kid with PTSD might seem overwhelming. You may be unclear about how to console children who are struggling with the repercussions of trauma. With the correct tools, parents may play a vital role in helping their kids manage PTSD.

A few approaches that you may support your kid with PTSD include:

Talk with a professional. Most parents and caregivers aren't educated on the best methods to assist a kid during a traumatic situation, but lots of mental health specialists are ready to help.

Acknowledge the painful experience. Pretending that things are OK isn't going to assist your kid. Let your kid speak about the experience and how it makes them feel as much or as little as they choose.

Talk with them about therapy. Some children and teenagers are reluctant to seek counseling or take medicine. Explain that therapy may make them feel better. Reassure them that there's nothing "wrong" with them and that many individuals require expert aid to feel better.

Keep a routine. Continue doing normal things with your kid, such as reading a bedtime tales or playing games together, or building new routines that involve additional activities your child likes.

Help them sleep. If your kid has difficulties sleeping, investigate strategies to help them feel comfortable. It's OK for your kid to sleep with a light on or to sleep in your room, at least for a short while. Talk with your kid's doctor about long-term measures to help your child sleep better.

Validate their sentiments. Let your youngster know that it's OK to weep and feel unhappy.

Empower your kid. Help your kid feel in control and powerful by allowing them to make decisions for themselves, such as what to dress or what they want to eat.

Assisted Recovery from Traumatic Events for Children and Adolescents

Cover visualization of NIMH publication Helping Children and Adolescents Cope with Disasters and Other Traumatic Events: What Parents, Rescue Workers, and the Community Can Do

Every year, children and teenagers face catastrophes and other stressful occurrences. Adolescents need assistance from family, friends, and reliable adults to deal with these situations.

How do children and teenagers react to stressful events?

After seeing or experiencing a traumatic incident like a natural disaster, violent crime, or a serious accident, it is common for kids and teens to feel a range of emotions.

Regardless of age, children and adolescents may:

Report suffering bodily difficulties such as stomachaches or headaches.

Have nightmares or other sleep issues, including refusing to go to bed.

Have difficulties focusing.

Lose interest in activities they generally like.

Have emotions of remorse for not avoiding injuries or fatalities.

Have thoughts of retribution.

Young children (age 5 and younger) may:

Cling to carers and/or weep and be emotional.

Have tantrums, or be irritated or disruptive.

Suddenly revert to activities such as bed-wetting and thumb-sucking.

Show greater fearfulness (for example, dread of the dark, monsters, or being alone).

Incorporate components of the painful incident into imagined play.

Older children (age 6 and older) and teenagers may:

Have issues at school.

Withdraw or become secluded from family and friends.

Avoid reminders of the occurrence.

Use drugs, alcohol, or cigarettes.

Be disruptive, impolite, or harmful.

Be furious or resentful.

Many of these responses are typical and will diminish with time. If these symptoms linger for more than a month, the family should contact a healthcare practitioner.

**What can adults do to help?**

How parents respond to trauma may substantially impact how children and adolescents react to trauma. When caregivers and family members take efforts to strengthen their own capacity to cope, they may offer greater care for others.

Caregivers and family members may assist by establishing a secure and supportive atmosphere, maintaining as calm as possible, and eliminating stress. Children and teenagers need to be assured that their family members love them and will do all in their power to look after them.

**Do:**

Ensure children and adolescents are protected and that their fundamental needs are handled.

Allow them to feel unhappy or weep.

Let them discuss, write, or draw images about the incident and their emotions.

Limit their exposure to recurrent news coverage about horrific incidents.

Let them sleep in your room (for a short period) or sleep with a light on if they are having problems sleeping.

Try to keep to rituals, such as reading bedtime tales, having supper together, and playing games.

Help them feel in control by allowing them to make certain choices for themselves, such as selecting their meals or picking out their clothing.

Pay attention to rapid changes in behaviors, speech, language usage, or intense emotions.

Contact a healthcare professional if new concerns emerge, especially if any of the following symptoms persist for more than a few weeks:

Having flashbacks (reliving the experience)

Having a beating heart and sweating

Being quickly startled

Being emotionally numb

Being exceedingly sad or depressed

**Don't:**

Expect children and teenagers to be bold or tough.

Make them discuss the incident before they are ready.

Get upset if they express strong emotions.

If they start acting out, peeing the bed, or sucking their thumb, become upset.

Make promises you can't make (such as "You will be OK tomorrow" or "You will go home soon.").

**For Yourself:**

Gently take three gentle breaths through your nose (one thousand one, one thousand two, and one thousand three) to comfortably fill your lungs all the way down to your abdomen.

Silently and softly murmur to yourself, "My body is filled with calmness." Exhale slowly (one-thousand one, one-thousand two, one-thousand three) via your mouth and comfortably empty your lungs all the way down to your belly.

Silently and softly remark to yourself, "My body is releasing the tension."

Repeat five times slowly and gently.

Do this as many times a day as required.

**For Children:**

Lead a youngster through a breathing exercise:

Let's try a different breathing technique that might help us relax our body.

Put one hand on your stomach

Okay, we are going to breathe in via our noses. When we breathe in, our stomachs will protrude outward as we fill up with a lot of air.

Then, we shall breathe out via our mouths. When we breathe out, our stomachs are going to pull in and up.

We are going to breathe in incredibly slowly while I count to three. I'm also going to count to three as we breathe out pretty slowly.

Let's try it together. Great job!"

**Make a game out of it:**

Use dish soap and a bubble wand to create bubbles.

Blow bubbles with chewing gum

Across the table, blow paper wads or cotton balls.

Tell a narrative where the kid helps you imitate a character who is taking deep breathes

## Chapter 4

# Discipline a Child with PTSD: Challenges, what to Avoid and What to Do

Knowing how to punish a kid with PTSD is a key element of parenting a child who has endured any form of trauma. Experiencing trauma, whether it was a single occurrence or repeated events, significantly impacts the child's emotions, thoughts, bodily responses, and behaviors and diminishes their capacity to deal in constructive ways.

Parents frequently feel helpless to assist their children and at a loss on how to reprimand them. Because understanding what not to do is just as important as knowing what to do, here are some mistakes to avoid while disciplining a traumatized child.

## The Challenges

Kids who have undergone trauma typically develop problematic habits. Being in perpetual survival mode and a condition of the fight, flee, or freeze, their brain is on alert for risks. What the brain wants, it typically finds, therefore children with PTSD are readily triggered. This leads to disturbing actions like:

Irritability

Clinginess

Frequent weeping bouts

Severe tantrums

Disobedience

Defiance

Refusal to listen or obey rules

Arguing

Talking back

Fighting

Getting into problems (both school and home)

Running away

Substance usage

Delinquency

Reckless, irresponsible behavior

These habits may be demanding, unpleasant, anxiety-provoking, and draining. Maybe you regularly feel at your wit's end. All the difficulties that come with discipline might interfere with your disciplining your kid. When you figure out how to discipline a child with PTSD, the process becomes easier, and your relationship with your child may improve.

## What Not to Do When Disciplining a Traumatized Child

When addressing the aforementioned issues, it's vital to bear in mind that they aren't purposeful but instead are responses to triggers that remind the kid of the trauma. It's normal for parents and other caregivers to take the bad behaviors personally; yet, no matter how it looks, the misbehavior often has nothing at all to do with the parents.

A key tip on how not to reprimand a kid with PTSD is to avoid taking the behavior personally. Remembering that your kid is working out of trauma rather than negative feelings toward you may help you stay calm and respond to your child rather than the outbursts.

When kids feel protected, loved, and understood, they react better to parental punishment. When disciplinary attempts overlook kids' needs for safety and security, they might endure setbacks that postpone healing and a lack of connectedness to their parents. Avoid these tactics and acts while punishing a kid with PTSD:

Forgetting to treat your child's emotions before dealing with the behavior

Instantly responding in wrath or frustration

Yelling

Touching, grabbing, or spanking your kid

Punishing—including any type of corporal punishment

Staring down the youngster or establishing lengthy eye contact (these are viewed as aggressiveness)

Ordering your youngster to talk/explain themselves

Interrupting and refusing to listen

Creating excessive expectations, either too high or too low Letting oneself be dragged into power conflicts, fighting and insisting on control

Using this list of what not to do will go far in disciplining a kid with PTSD. Avoiding these behaviors can help you kindly educate your kid about what behaviors you find undesirable.

**What to Do**

Seek to understand your child's PTSD symptoms and responses to numerous triggers. In this manner, you may more easily avoid destructive disciplining measures and apply a constructive, kind approach that helps children progressively recover from their traumatic experience(s). These traits and acts go a long way in making youngsters feel loved and protected when disciplined:

Patience

Gentleness

A calm, quiet temperament

Availability when your kid wants to chat

Willingness to offer your kid some options and control

Use of natural, rational, and short-term consequences

Realistic expectations for your kid

Finally, the way you perceive your kid is vital. It influences how you engage with children and determines your approach to discipline.

In fact, the main thing to avoid when disciplining a child with PTSD is to see just their bad behavior and let it define who they are.

## Chapter 5

# Effective Parenting Strategies for Teens with PTSD

Parenting an adolescent with PTSD requires a unique set of skills and strategies to support their rehabilitation and recovery. In this section, we will examine effective parenting strategies that can help create a supportive and nurturing environment for adolescents with PTSD.

These strategies include active listening and validation techniques, positive reinforcement and encouragement, as well as establishing realistic expectations and goals. By implementing these approaches, parents can play a vital role in their teenager's voyage toward healing and resilience.

## Active Listening and Validation Techniques

One of the most fundamental aspects of effective parenting for adolescents with PTSD is active listening. Active listening entails lending complete attention to your adolescent when they express their thoughts, emotions, and experiences. It requires setting aside distractions and demonstrating genuine interest in what they have to say.

When engaging in active listening, it is essential to exercise empathy and validation. Validate your teenager's emotions and experiences by acknowledging their feelings and providing reassurance that their reactions are normal given the circumstances. Avoid dismissing or minimizing their emotions, as this can undermine their sense of safety and trust.

Active listening also entails establishing a non-judgmental space where your adolescent feels secure expressing their thoughts and concerns. Use open-ended queries to encourage them to elaborate on their experiences, and avoid interrupting or offering immediate solutions.

Instead, focus on comprehending their perspective and offering support.

## Positive Reinforcement and Encouragement

Positive reinforcement and encouragement are potent instruments in nurturing a teenager's self-esteem and motivation. Recognize and acknowledge their efforts and achievements, no matter how modest. Offer specific commendation that highlights their strengths and resilience. This helps them develop confidence and reinforces positive behaviors.

Incorporate rewards and incentives into their daily routine as a means of reinforcing positive behaviors and progress. Celebrate milestones and accomplishments, and remind your adolescent of the progress they have made on their rehabilitation voyage. However, it is crucial to establish a balance by avoiding excessive pressure or unrealistic expectations, as this can contribute to additional tension.

## Setting Realistic Expectations and Goals

Setting realistic expectations and objectives is crucial for adolescents with PTSD. Understand that their journey of rehabilitation may not follow a linear path, and there may be setbacks along the way. Avoid comparing their progress to others or imposing unrealistic standards. Instead, focus on their individual development and celebrate their resilience.

Work collaboratively with your adolescent to establish achievable objectives. Break larger duties into smaller, manageable steps, and celebrate their progress at each milestone. Encourage them to develop a sense of agency and autonomy by involving them in the goal-setting process. This promotes a sense of ownership and empowerment, enabling them to take command of their recovery.

While establishing objectives, it is essential to be flexible and adaptable. Recognize that their requirements and abilities may vacillate, and adjust expectations accordingly. Offer support and guidance as they navigate challenges, but also allow them the space to learn from their experiences and develop problem-solving skills.

In addition to setting objectives related to their rehabilitation journey, encourage your adolescent to engage in activities they appreciate and find meaningful. Hobbies, creative pursuits, and social interactions can contribute to their overall well-being and provide a sense of pleasure and purpose.

In conclusion, effective parental strategies for adolescents with PTSD involve active listening, validation techniques, positive reinforcement, encouragement, and establishing realistic expectations and goals. By implementing these strategies, parents can create a supportive and nurturing environment that promotes their teenager's rehabilitation and resilience.

Remember, each teenager's experience with PTSD is unique, and it is crucial to adapt these strategies to suit their individual requirements. Seek guidance from mental health professionals and utilize trusted resources to enhance your understanding and further develop your parenting skills. With your unwavering support and commitment, your adolescent can navigate the challenges of PTSD and emerge stronger on their path to recovery.

Active listening and validation techniques provide a firm foundation for developing trust and connection with your adolescent. By actively listening and validating their experiences, you create a secure space for them to express themselves without fear of judgment or dismissal. This foster open communication and strengthens the parent-teenager relationship, allowing for a deeper understanding of their needs and challenges.

In addition to active listening, positive reinforcement and encouragement play a vital role in bolstering your teenager's self-esteem and motivation. Recognizing their efforts and accomplishments, no matter how minor, helps them recognize their own strengths and progress. By offering specific praise and highlighting their resilience, you instill confidence and empower them to continue their voyage toward healing.

However, it's crucial to establish a balance between delivering positive reinforcement and averting excessive pressure. Be mindful of setting realistic expectations that take into consideration the unique challenges your adolescent experiences due to PTSD. Adjust your expectations as required, considering their individual progress and circumstances. Remember that healing is a gradual process, and setbacks are a normal part of the voyage.

Setting achievable objectives is an effective way to provide structure and direction for your adolescent. Break down larger objectives into smaller, manageable actions to make them more attainable. Collaborate with your adolescent in the goal-setting process, allowing them to have a voice and ownership in their own recovery. By involving them, you encourage autonomy and empower them to take an active role in their rehabilitation.

Flexibility is essential when establishing objectives for adolescents with PTSD. Understand that their requirements and abilities may vary over time, and be prepared to adapt your approach accordingly. Be supportive and provide guidance as they navigate challenges, but also give them space to learn and develop their own problem-solving skills. This helps foster resilience and independence.

While it's essential to concentrate on their rehabilitation journey, don't neglect the significance of activities they appreciate and find meaningful. Encourage your adolescent to engage in pursuits, creative outlets, and social interactions that bring them pleasure. These activities can provide a sense of purpose and balance, promoting overall well-being.

In implementing these effective parenting strategies, it's essential to be patient, compassionate, and understanding. Educate yourself about PTSD and seek guidance from mental health professionals who can offer specialized support. Remember that you are not alone in this voyage, and reaching out for assistance is a sign of fortitude.

In summation, effective parental strategies for adolescents with PTSD involve active listening, validation, positive reinforcement, encouragement, and establishing realistic expectations and goals.

By employing these strategies, you create a supportive and nurturing environment that promotes your teenager's rehabilitation and development. Remember to adapt these strategies to suit their individual requirements and seek professional guidance when necessary. With your unwavering support, your adolescent can navigate the challenges of PTSD and emerge stronger, constructing a brighter future filled with resilience and hope.

## Chapter 6

## Tips for Teachers

Younger children could continually re-enact portions of their trauma via play or draw it out, they might become clingier, acquire more general anxieties of perceived hazards (e.g. the dark, animals, and being alone) and can look more oppositional – asserting greater control over their settings.

### Be alert and observe

Keep aware of who in your class has been exposed to traumatic experiences. Be aware of and watch out for typical signs of PTSD. As avoidance is one of the key symptoms of PTSD, it may be quite difficult to identify. Be mindful of the variations in symptoms throughout younger children and teenagers. Bear in mind that certain symptoms of PTSD (e.g. increased irritation) might appear like something else (e.g. being bad).

Children who have encountered traumatic situations might be readily 'triggered' and upset by reminders of such events. Have an awareness of reminders that can function as triggers so that you can plan solutions to enable children to manage, in the moment. Triggers will be different for each kid and will frequently closely link to the incident they encountered, while at other times they might be more discrete. For example, a loud door bang or a certain day.

**Grounding**

Grounding approaches may be used to link children to the here and now. They often demand youngsters pay attention to their five senses. '5,4', '3,2,1' is a fairly simple one that asks children to list five things they can see, four things they can feel, three things they hear, two things they can smell, and one item they can taste. Practice grounding exercises as a whole class to avoid singling out children who have endured trauma.

Other grounding strategies include practicing quiet breathing, muscular relaxation, listening to music, and coloring. It's crucial to practice these tactics even when they are not required, so that they may be called upon more rapidly when they are needed. Lots of wonderful grounding films may be available online, for example, Belly Breathing with Elmo from Sesame Street on YouTube.

**Calming Corner and Coping Box**

If feasible, locate a location in your classroom where children may go when they start to feel triggered. Fill it with sensory objects such as blankets, pillows, and lights. Add a coping box stocked with sensory play materials such as play dough, fidget toys, and lavender bags. Ensure youngsters know how and when they may utilize the soothing nook. Having a signal or code which they may use to let you know that they need to utilize the coping corner might be beneficial.

For example, a 'time-out' card that they may give you. Some youngsters will need your support to determine when they may need the soothing zone.

## Then Versus Now

Another important strategy to react to children's discomfort might be to enable them to identify distinctions between 'then', the day of their trauma, and 'now', today when they are presented with triggers. For example, you may remark 'Then the loud bang was a gunshot, today it was a door slamming, and you are safe'. Encourage youngsters to do this themselves too, they may find it beneficial to jot out the changes between then and today.

## Reflective listening

It is frequently considered that sharing traumatic situations might make PTSD symptoms worse, although data show the reverse is true; talking can enable youngsters to overcome suffering, even if it is hard at first. Unless children are questioned about stressful situations, PTSD symptoms are equally likely to be ignored. Children also have vivid imaginations, and without addressing unpleasant incidents, can be assuming the worst. Offer children the chance to talk about what is bothering them, when they are calm. Be careful to indicate that you encourage communication when they would want, since children with symptoms of PTSD may frequently avoid talking about their issues because they do not want to hurt others (particularly those who could also have been impacted by the incident too).

Let them know a designated person who they can go to. Keep in mind that it is natural for youngsters to find it extremely difficult to talk about painful incidents, and do not press them. Be patient throughout debates.

Show that you have listened to them, confirm your knowledge of what they are saying, and validate their feelings. Remain calm while conducting these dialogues. Reinforce what is known now; that the terrible experience has come to a conclusion, and that the kid is secure.

### Challenge misunderstandings

although children are feeling harmful beliefs such as that they were to blame for the traumatic incident, that they did something wrong or shameful throughout, or that the occurrence (although uncommon) is likely to happen again, it might be beneficial to counter their thoughts with what is known.

For example, inform them that they were not to blame, that they did everything they could at the time that their feelings are natural and reasonable, and that the occurrence is unlikely to happen again. Only confront misconceptions. It is crucial to stay honest with children about what did happen so that misconceptions might be eliminated.

### Limit reassurance giving

Monitor and restrict how much comfort you are offering youngsters about their fears. Although it is normal to want to provide comfort, it might perpetuate challenges in the long term. Instead, ask youngsters what they know now that they did not know at the time of their trauma, and what they can do to feel better.

## Manage difficult behaviors

Traumatized youngsters might frequently act in a manner that's disruptive and deemed 'naughty' by adults. It's crucial to remember, particularly for younger children, greater levels of irritability, rage and aggressiveness are some of the most prevalent signs of post-traumatic stress. Set clear and consistent standards of conduct as well as penalties for not fulfilling them. The focus of the expectations should be on what you want to see, for example 'kind hands', rather than what you do not want to see, for example, 'hitting others'. Consequences should also be rational and fair, not punitive.

## Establish and adhere to everyday routines

Following a regular pattern makes children's days more predictable and so promotes their feeling of safety. Support youngsters to follow visual schedules and allow them the option to make more choices about their day to give them more of a feeling of control.

### Aid concentration

These youngsters are likely to struggle to focus on activities, particularly in the hectic classroom. Support kids to remain focused by providing information in numerous forms, reducing job instructions down into smaller, more achievable, stages, and seating youngsters in locations with fewer distractions.

### Encourage 'reclaiming life'

Low mood and a lack of enthusiasm to participate in previously loved activities are also frequent after a trauma. Look out for this during break times and with extra-curricular activities. Encourage youngsters to continue to participate in previously appreciated activities, even if they don't feel like it.

## Promote strengths via delivering praise and prizes

It might be tempting to concentrate on the negatives with these children, but it is crucial to focus more on the child's strengths. Acknowledging, praising, and rewarding them for obeying class rules and adopting coping methods may be a simple, yet extremely successful approach for instructors to utilize.

## Foster a whole class approach to promoting safety

Teach broad ideas on how to be safe, as part of the curriculum. For example, educate children on basic self-care (e.g. sleep hygiene and body ownership principles), to identify trustworthy people that they may turn to when feeling uncomfortable and who to call in an emergency. Remind children that their parents and caregivers are responsible for protecting their safety too and that if they are unclear about what to do in an uncertain circumstance, a trusted adult should be able to assist.

### Communicate with others

Remember to converse with parents and caregivers about how their children are doing. Inform them of challenges you detect, since children may be more avoidant of informing their caretakers that they are suffering. Ask parents and caregivers about recognized triggers and ways that they are employing to control symptoms at home. Consistency is crucial – so share these top tips with them too! Bear in mind that depending on the traumatic experience, parents might be traumatized themselves. It is also conceivable that the danger is continuous and thus it will be vital to speak with appropriate specialists to address protection.

### Monitor symptoms and refer on

Remember that you are not supposed to be a therapist. Monitor how long symptoms remain. If they persist for more than one month after the traumatic incident happens, professional help is recommended, and we urge that youngsters consult their GP. PTSD almost seldom resolves itself on its own without specialized assistance.

## Chapter 7

## The Aftermath of PTSD In Children

PTSD or post-traumatic stress disorder is a devastating mental condition that prohibits a person from enjoying their life to the fullest. They look remote and unapproachable when it comes to the genesis of their PTSD. Adults grow apathetic to others and may easily slide into other mental diseases like depression. However, PTSD doesn't only target adults. If ignored, childhood PTSD is just as prevalent as adult PTSD and has the potential to ruin a child's future.

## What Takes Place If Children with PTSD Are Not Treated?

Even while PTSD may be damaging to adults, it may be even more so for a young child or teenager who are still in their formative years. If it isn't addressed, then children with PTSD will wind up carrying their mental disease till adulthood. It might be difficult if not impossible to cure from then on therefore it's better to receive aid as soon as possible. Some of the things that a youngster could carry over to adulthood include:

## Social Awkwardness

others with PTSD tend to block others out of their life, regardless of who they are. That implies that they will end up having problems establishing and maintaining friends, business partners, and even love partners. This will lead them to have problems in life since without these a person might slide into vices or even more serious mental diseases.

## Difficulty Trusting Other People

This is one of the rarer effects of PTSD in adolescents. It mostly depends on whether the traumatic event was imparted to the child by someone they trust. If this is the case, then such individuals will make an effort to keep others at a distance since they think that others will only betray their confidence. Similar to social awkwardness, but much worse because they deliberately cut themselves apart from others.

## A Predisposition for Other Mental Disorders

PTSD, like many other mental disorders, damages a person's psyche and can make it simpler for them to develop other mental disorders. PTSD in minors can easily cause anxiety disorders, and depression to become a significant negative factor in a person's future. It's a pernicious cycle that's difficult to stop.

## Slower and Damaged Cognitive Development

The brain is one of the most essential sections of the body. It's what makes you, you. Children experiencing PTSD will have diminished cerebral development when compared to a typical child. This causes them to have a delayed capability to learn, lower general IQ, memory difficulties, impaired social and emotional responses, and a defensive personality. They can all make it very challenging to interact with a youngster who has PTSD. It can very easily result in a great deal more maturity-related issue.

**What Can You Do?**

Taking a child with childhood PTSD to a qualified specialist is the best thing you can do as a parent or relative. They'll have the ability to recommend treatments like counseling and medicine. This aids a youngster in overcoming their PTSD and enables them to lead more fruitful adult lives.

Help your child feel secure. They may need extra attention, solace, and care from you for a while.

Ensure your kid is at ease. They can join you in taking a few deep breaths. Inhale as you count to three. Exhale while counting to five.

Do something together that you like. Trauma might make it tougher to experience the joyful feelings that normally aid kids' recharge. Play, laugh, appreciate nature, produce music or art, cook. These exercises may relieve stress and increase your child's resilience.

Reassure your youngster. Tell them they can overcome this. And that you are there to assist.

Let your kid's doctor know what your child has gone through. Get a referral to a mental health expert (such as a psychiatrist, psychologist, or mental health counselor who specializes in trauma treatment).

Tell your kid's instructor that your youngster went suffered a trauma. Kids with PTSD may have greater problems concentrating on homework. Ask for your kid to have additional support or more time to finish homework if they need it for a long.

Printed in Great Britain
by Amazon